You Are Extra-Ordinary

DECLARING GOD'S EMPOWERING WORD OVER YOUR CHILDREN

Written and photographed by
ANGELA FORKER

Copyright © 2025 by Angela Forker
All rights reserved. No part of this book may be reproduced in any form without permission in writing from the publisher, except by a reviewer who may quote brief passages in a review or article.

Scripture taken from the International Children's Bible®.
Copyright © 1986, 1988, 2015 by Thomas Nelson. Used by permission. All rights reserved.

Scripture quotations taken from the New Life Version (NLV).
Copyright © 1969, 2003 by Christian Literature International. Used by permission.

Scripture quotations from the Berean Standard Bible (BSB).
Copyright © 2016, 2020 by Bible Hub. Used by permission. All rights reserved worldwide.

Scripture quotations taken from the Holy Bible, New International Version®, NIV®.
Copyright © 1973, 1978, 1984, 2011 by Biblica, Inc.™ Used by permission. All rights reserved worldwide.

Scripture taken from the Contemporary English Version®.
Copyright © 1991, 1992, 1995 by American Bible Society. Used by permission.

Scripture quotations taken from the Holy Bible, New International Reader's Version®, NIrV®.
Copyright © 1995, 1996, 1998 by Biblica, Inc.™ Used by permission. All rights reserved worldwide.

Scripture quotations are from The Holy Bible, English Standard Version® (ESV®).
Copyright © 2001 by Crossway, a publishing ministry of Good News Publishers. Used by permission. All rights reserved.

Scripture quotations taken from the Holy Bible, New Living Translation, NLT®.
Copyright © 1996, 2004, 2015 by Tyndale House Foundation. Used by permission of Tyndale House Publishers, Inc., Carol Stream, Illinois 60188. All rights reserved.

Scripture taken from the New King James Version®.
Copyright © 1982 by Thomas Nelson. Used by permission. All rights reserved.

Published by Angela Forker
Printed in the United States of America

ISBN: 979-8-9933787-1-8
First Edition

Cover design and photography by Angela Forker

To my three beautiful daughters—
Candace, Charity and Christina:
May God's Word guide you as you raise your children.

To my precious grandchildren—
Ricky, Daisy, Antony, Juliette, Zoey, Jonas, Zion and Chloe:
May you always follow God's great plan for your life.

You are extra-ordinary!

Thank you to each of my wonderful grandchildren for being a part of this book—
you are such a gift to me!
A special thank you, also, to my amazing friends who joined in:
Chiagozie, Chidera, Chiemeka, Cortez, Cossette, Lila, Marisella, Patrick and Sophie—
you helped make this book extra-special!

Note to Parents and Grandparents

Thank you for choosing *You Are Extra-Ordinary: Declaring God's Empowering Word Over Your Children*! The longer I live, the more I treasure God's Word and the power of speaking it aloud. The words we speak over our children can shape the course of their lives—bringing hope instead of despair, and building a strong sense of identity instead of feelings of worthlessness.

This book was created to help you speak words of life, love, affirmation and empowerment—into your children's lives. You can use it in whatever way works best for your family:

- **For younger children**: Read the titles aloud and then speak the personalized Bible verses over their lives. You can talk about the photos and verses together or simply enjoy them as a picture book.

- **For older children**: Use one devotion a day. You may find it helpful to begin with the title and personalized Bible verse, then continue with the devotion.

- **For independent reading**: Older children may enjoy reading the devotions on their own.

No matter how you choose to use this devotional, my prayer is that it will be a powerful tool to help you speak God's Empowering Word into your children's hearts. As you declare His promises and read these devotions together, may God's Word become living and active in them (Hebrews 4:12), and may not one word return empty (Isaiah 55:11).

Who knows what God may do through your children!

In Christ's love,
Angela Forker

You Are Important

Have you ever felt like you are less important because you are a child? Sometimes it feels that way, especially when adults are busy. But the Bible says, *"You are young, but do not let anyone treat you as if you were not important."*

To God, you are very important—just as important as any adult! Being a child is special. You see things in a different way. You have a pure heart. You have faith that can believe God for anything.

I pray that God will help you be like Him. Be like Him *"with your words, with the way you live, with your love, with your faith, and with your pure life."* When you do this, God will use your life to show others His love and to help them find Jesus.

You may be young, but your faith is strong. Always remember—you are important to God. He wants to use *you* to do *great things* in this world!

You are young, but do not let anyone treat you as if you were not important. Be an example to show the believers how they should live. Show them with your words, with the way you live, with your love, with your faith, and with your pure life. (1 Timothy 4:12 ICB)

You Are God's Masterpiece

Do you know that you are God's masterpiece? That means you are His very best work of art! When God made you, He didn't make any mistakes. That's because He thought really hard about how He was going to make you.

He thought carefully about every little detail—your smile, your laugh, your eyes, even the way you think! You are unique—there is no one else in the whole wide world exactly like you. You are special!

A very long time ago—before you were even born—God made a plan for your life. It's not just any plan. It's a good plan! It's filled with love, joy and all the good things that He wants you to do.

When you follow God with all your heart, He will guide you. When you let Him work in your life, He will help you grow strong in your faith. And as you grow, you will get to see all the amazing things He has planned for you.

God is looking for someone who will bring His love, His kindness and His light to this world. Will you let Him use your life to do those good things?

For we are God's masterpiece. He has created us anew in Christ Jesus, so we can do the good things he planned for us long ago. (Ephesians 2:10 NLV)

You Are an Overcomer

Do you know that you are an overcomer? That means no matter what difficulties come your way, you are victorious—you will win! All because Jesus is inside your heart. His power is greater than any other power. When you speak the name of Jesus, He pushes the evil away!

That means you don't have to be afraid. Not of monsters. Not of the dark. Not even the devil—because God's power is *always* greater!

When you feel scared, remember this verse from 1 John 4:4..."*greater is He who is in you (Jesus) than he who is in the world (the devil).*"

You can even make it personal just for you and speak it out loud, "greater is He who is in *me* than he who is in the world." If you'd like, you can also add these words... "Jesus is inside me. I will walk in faith, not in fear. I will *not* be afraid."

Never forget—Jesus' great power is inside you. You don't have to be afraid. You are victorious. You are an overcomer!

You, little children, are from God and have overcome them, because greater is He who is in you than he who is in the world. (1 John 4:4 BSB)

Greater is HE who is in you than he who is in the world

1 John 4:4

You Are Always Heard

Do you ever feel like no one hears you, even when you're really trying to say something important? Sometimes you might feel like there is no one who really hears what you are trying to say—kind of like a person who is trying to call someone important on the phone, but no one answers. Sometimes there's a message—or even a kind of robot that answers! Other times they have to wait and wait and wait to finally talk to someone.

But God is different. When you call out to Him in prayer, He says that He *will* answer you. You don't need a phone. There's no busy signal, no robot to talk to, no waiting. God promises to answer you every time, saying, *"Here am I!"* He is always ready to hear about what is making you happy or sad. And when you need help, He will be there for you—day or night!

So call out to God every day. Just talk to Him like you would talk to a friend. And when you do, you can know He will always hear you and answer you!

Then you will call, and the LORD will answer; you will cry for help, and he will say: Here am I. (Isaiah 58:9 NIV)

You Are Loved

Do you try to fit in so your friends will like you? Maybe you wear the same clothes, say the same words, or act the same way.

You want to feel loved and accepted. But if you do wrong things to be accepted, it might make your friends happy, but it can also hide Jesus in you.

Here's the good news: you are already loved! God has chosen you as His own special child. He wants you to share His love by putting on kindness, gentleness, patience, thankfulness, forgiveness, and peace—like you put on your clothes each day. When you do, people will see that you follow Jesus.

Instead of trying to be more like your friends, ask Jesus to help you be more like Him. Be brave. Be different. Show His love.

God loves you and has chosen *you* to live for Him and help others find Him!

God loves you and has chosen you as his own special people. (Colossians 3:12 CEV) So put on tender mercy and kindness as if they were your clothes. Don't be proud. Be gentle and patient. Put up with one another. Forgive one another... And over all these good things put on love... Let the peace that Christ gives rule in your hearts... And be thankful. (Colossians 3:12-15 NIrV)

You Are Made Clean

Have you ever gotten so dirty that you thought you could never get clean? That's when you get in a big sudsy bath. Sometimes you have to really scrub!

But what if your heart feels dirty? Maybe you've done something you know God didn't want you to do. Those are called sins. And sometimes you might even wonder if some of your sins are too big for God to forgive.

Here's the good news: God made a way for everyone to be clean! It's not through soap and bubbles; it's through the blood of His Son, Jesus.

Wait...did I just say blood? Jesus' *blood* can make you clean?

When Jesus died on the cross, His blood was spilled. That blood has the power to wash away the sins of *anyone* who believes in Him. There is no sin too big for God to forgive and no person too bad for Him to save.

So if you've done something wrong, you can ask Jesus to forgive you and make you clean. Never forget: the blood of Jesus cleanses you from *all* sin!

But if we walk in the light, as he is in the light, we have fellowship with one another, and the blood of Jesus his Son cleanses us from all sin. (1 John 1:7 ESV)

You Are a God-Seeker

Do you like to play hide-and-seek? One person counts while the others hide. The seeker tries to find all of the players who are hiding.

When it comes to seeking God, it works a little differently. God is always looking for us. Some people hide from God, but others are looking for Him—and actually want to be found! That is what God wants. He tells us that if we seek Him, we *will* find Him! It might not always be easy, though. There might be other things that get our attention while we're trying to find God. That's why He says we need to seek Him with *all* our heart.

Do you know how to seek God? Some of the ways you can seek Him are by praying, reading your Bible and going to church. You can also take time to be quiet while you're praying and ask God to speak to you. When you do, you might hear His still, small voice. It's like a whisper in your heart.

I pray that you will never hide from or run away from God. Instead, I pray that you will run to Him—that you will seek Him with all of your heart. Because God promises that if you seek Him, you *will* find Him!

You will seek me and find me when you seek me with all your heart. (Jeremiah 29:13 NIV)

You Are Showered with Blessings

Have you ever thought about all that God has done for you? Let's think about the beautiful world God created for us. He filled it with tall mountains, splashing waterfalls and sandy beaches. He covered it with amazing plants, trees and flowers. And don't forget about all the different bugs and animals! To make it even better, He gave us colorful sunrises and sunsets. He didn't have to do any of this, but He did it because He loves us and wanted the world we live in to be extra-special!

But He didn't just give us a beautiful world to live in. He also gives us rain from heaven and plenty of food to eat! And as if that weren't enough, He gave us His Son, Jesus—and He also fills our hearts with joy!

At times we don't think about how much God has done for us. We forget that every blessing comes from Him—because of His kindness and His love!

Think about all that God does for you—every single day. He does so much for you—and He's going to keep doing it—because He *loves* you! Every sunrise. Every meal. Every smile in your heart. Each one is a gift from Him. Take a little time today to thank Him for all of His kindness in your life.

He has shown kindness by giving you rain from heaven and crops in their seasons; he provides you with plenty of food and fills your hearts with joy. (Acts 14:17 NIV)

You Are Wise

Do you do something just because "everyone else" is doing it? Wise people don't follow the crowd. They don't rush into things. They think first. They ask, "What will happen if I do this?"

Wise people also pray before making a big decision because they know God knows what is best for His children.

You can be wise too. If you look to God, He will help you know what is the best thing to do.

So before you follow the crowd and do something that could hurt you or someone else, stop for a moment. Ask yourself, "If I do this, what will happen to me? What will happen to others?"

When you need to make an important choice, always take some time to pray: "God, please show me what I should do."

God loves you and has placed His wisdom inside you. Don't rush. Take time to think and pray. Let God's wisdom guide you in all you do.

Wise people think before they act (Proverbs 13:16 NLT)

You Are Unmovable

Is your house built on the rock? Jesus said that a wise person builds their house on solid rock. When the storms come, their house stays strong. But a foolish person builds their house on the sand. When the rain pours down and the waters rise, their house goes splat!

Your life is like a house. What kind of house do you have?

Is your house built on the sand? That's like a person who chooses not to obey Jesus. When the storms of life come—hard things like sadness, sickness, or trouble—their house isn't strong. It might even come crashing down!

But if your house is built on Jesus, the solid rock, then no matter what happens, your house will stand. The rains of sadness might come. The waters of sickness might rise. The winds of temptation might try to shake you. But because your life is built on Jesus, the solid rock, your house will. not. fall.

So take time every day to pray and read God's Word. Ask God to help you listen to Him and obey Him. With Jesus, you are strong and unmovable!

Anyone who hears and obeys these teachings of mine is like a wise person who built a house on solid rock. Rain poured down, rivers flooded, and winds beat against that house. But it was built on solid rock, and so it did not fall. (Matthew 7:24-25 CEV)

When you *hear & obey* the teachings of **JESUS** you are like a *wise person* who built a house on **SOLID ROCK.** If the rain pours down, if the rivers flood, if the winds beat against your house *it will not fall.*
Matthew 7:24-25

You Are Saved

Do you know that God loves you so much that He gave His only Son for you? God is a loving Father. He made you and this beautiful world. His plan was that we would love Him and one day live with Him forever in heaven.

But all of us have sinned. Sin is when we disobey God. Since God is holy—perfect and without sin—He cannot let sin into heaven. That's why God sent His Son, Jesus. Jesus was born on earth and taught people about His Father in heaven. Then He gave His life on the cross for us. But it didn't end there—after three days, God raised Jesus from the dead by His great power!

Because of Jesus, our sins can be forgiven. God's gift is for everyone—no matter who you are, where you come from, or what you've done. If you believe in Jesus, you can be forgiven and have eternal life.

Would you like to invite Jesus into your heart today? You can say this prayer: "Dear Jesus, thank You for loving me so much that You gave Your life for me. I know I have sinned. Please forgive me. I believe You died on the cross for me and that God raised You from the dead. I put my trust in You. Be my Savior and my Lord. Help me live for You every day. In Jesus' name, Amen."

For God so loved the world, that he gave his only Son, that whoever believes in him should not perish but have eternal life. (John 3:16 ESV)

You Are a New Creation

Have you been made into a new creation? If you have asked Jesus to come into your heart, then this is the beginning of something new!

Think about a butterfly. It starts out as a caterpillar, crawling on the ground. I wonder if a caterpillar ever gets tired of only crawling—if it dreams of being something more.

One day it feels very tired of its old life. So it goes away to a quiet place all by itself. It looks like nothing is happening, but inside the cocoon (or chrysalis), something amazing is going on! When the caterpillar comes out, it's not the same anymore. It is a new creation—a butterfly!

That's a picture of what happens when we come to Jesus. Our old way of living is gone. No more crawling in sin. When we give our lives to Jesus, He changes us. And then we find out...we can fly! We can rise above sin and the things of this world. We are free to live the brand-new life Jesus gives us.

So keep living as the new creation Jesus made you to be. He has a wonderful plan for your life! Follow Him every day. And remember—there's nothing for you back in that old cocoon. You are a new creation!

Therefore, if anyone is in Christ, he is a new creation; old things have passed away; behold, all things have become new. (2 Corinthians 5:17 NKJV)

You Are a Healthy Thinker

God gave us an amazing brain that can think of all kinds of things! Some of the things we think about are really good. God loves it when we read His Word and then think about how it fits into our life.

But sometimes, instead of good thoughts, we let wrong ones fill our mind. Maybe we think about lies, mean things or things God doesn't want us to do. Sometimes we think too much about things that make us afraid. These thoughts are like junk food for your mind. If you eat too much junk food, your body feels bad. In the same way, if you fill your mind with junk, your heart and mind won't be healthy.

That's why God tells us to think about things that are true, pure, right, holy, friendly, and proper. These are like healthy food for your mind. When you fill your mind with good, healthy thoughts, your mind will be strong.

If you've been thinking about wrong or unhealthy things, ask God to help you fill your mind with good things—things that are worthy of praise. Then your thoughts will make God happy, and He will fill you with His peace.

Finally, my friends, keep your minds on whatever is true, pure, right, holy, friendly, and proper. Don't ever stop thinking about what is truly worthwhile and worthy of praise. (Philippians 4:8 CEV)

You Are Beautiful

Do you want to be beautiful? (If you're a boy, you might say handsome!) I'll tell you a secret: what you see in the mirror isn't a true reflection of how beautiful you are. Your real beauty is what's inside your heart.

When God looks for beauty, He doesn't see the same things other people see. People look at the outside, but God looks at the heart. Why? Because many people look amazing on the outside, but inside they are full of meanness, jealousy, selfishness or hate. So who is really more beautiful?

The truth is, someone others might call "ugly" could actually be one of the kindest, most thoughtful and generous people around. If you compare that person with someone who is popular and good-looking but filled with hate, the one with the beautiful heart wins every time.

True beauty comes from deep within. That's what God is looking for. So even though it can be fun to make yourself look nice on the outside, never forget to take care of the inside too. Ask Jesus to make your heart beautiful first. When your heart is beautiful, it shines through you for everyone to see. And best of all, God will choose *you* because of your beautiful heart.

But the Lord said... "The Lord does not look at the things people look at. People look at the outward appearance, but the Lord looks at the heart." (1 Samuel 16:7 NIV)

You Are Pure in Heart

Are you careful to protect your heart? Everything you think, say and do comes from it.

If you fill your heart with good things—the things God loves—then goodness will flow out of you. But if you let in sin, evil or anything against God, it will lead you to make bad choices.

That's why the Bible says, *"Above all else, guard your heart!"* What's inside your heart decides who you really are.

So be wise about what you watch and read, and the music you listen to. Each day, ask God to help you turn away from what is wrong so your thoughts, words and actions stay pure.

Open your heart to Jesus and let Him show you anything that isn't pleasing to Him. If He points out something, confess it to Him. He will forgive you and make you clean again.

As you walk with Jesus, He will help you guard your heart so it stays pure. When your heart is clean, His goodness will flow out of you for others to see.

Above all else, guard your heart, for everything you do flows from it. (Proverbs 4:23 NIV)

You Are Trusting

Do you ever feel frustrated when someone tells you, "...when you're older"? You try to be patient, but you want to do those exciting things now! You feel like you're in a cage, kept from being able to do or have anything fun.

The first thing to remember is that your parents are *for* you—they're not against you. They aren't trying to keep you from doing or having all the fun stuff; they just want what's best for you. It is their job to look out for you—to be sure that you are safe.

It can be the same way with God. You might want something now, but God knows that it's not the right timing. He wants to make everything beautiful for you, but it has to happen *His* way and in *His* timing.

That's why, in everything in life, God wants you to be patient. He wants you to trust Him—and trust your parents. He wants you to wait on Him. You may not always understand what God is doing, but He sees the whole picture, even when you can't. Later, when you look back, you will see that His way was best. God makes everything beautiful—at just the right time.

Yet God has made everything beautiful for its own time. He has planted eternity in the human heart, but even so, people cannot see the whole scope of God's work from beginning to end. (Ecclesiastes 3:11 NLT)

GOD MAKES EVERYTHING *beautiful* for you IN ITS TIME
Ecclesiastes 3:11

You Are Meant to Shine

Did you know you were called to be a light in this world? Without Jesus, the world is in darkness. There is no hope. If you are a Christian, you are called to be a light. This happens when you grow closer to Jesus and become more like Him. His light shines through you, helping others come to Him.

At times you may feel like no one else wants to live for Jesus. You might even be tempted to hide your light. But Jesus says to let your light shine for *all* to see. When you do, it helps others see His reflection in you, like a mirror.

You may also wonder if your tiny light makes a difference. Think about a little flashlight. If you turn it on in the middle of the day, will anyone see it? Probably not. But what if you turn it on at night? Even a tiny light will shine brightly. If you're worried that the world is getting dark, remember—that's when your light is needed most. That's when your light will *really* be seen!

Your light is so important in this dark world. Let it shine for all to see!

You are the light of the world. A town built on a hill cannot be hidden. Neither do people light a lamp and put it under a bowl. Instead they put it on its stand, and it gives light to everyone in the house. In the same way, let your light shine before others, that they may see your good deeds and glorify your Father in heaven. (Matthew 5:14-16 NIV)

You Are Going to Be Alright

Are you worried about your future? Sometimes it feels scary when we hear about all the bad things in the world. If we listen to the news too much, it can make us afraid! Sometimes the news makes things sound extra big and scary so that more people will watch or listen. That isn't always good, is it? It can make people's hearts feel full of fear. But God doesn't want us to be afraid. He wants us to have faith—and to trust Him.

It's okay to know what's going on in the world, but it's even more important to know this: God is always with you. He will protect you. And no matter what is happening around you, God will stay right by your side and help you through it.

This is what God says about you: "There is *surely* a *future hope* for you." And He doesn't stop there. He goes on to say, "your hope *will not* be cut off." You will always have hope! Why? Because you have Jesus. No matter what is going on—with your family, at your school or in this world—you. have. hope.

So hold onto Jesus—don't give up! Because a bright future is waiting for you!

There is surely a future hope for you, and your hope will not be cut off. (Proverbs 23:18 NIV)

there is **SURELY** *a future* **HOPE** *for you* and your **HOPE** *will* **NOT** *be cut off*
Proverbs 23:18

You Are a Child of God

Do you live like a child of God? God is your Father in heaven, and His love for you is amazing! He loves you so much that He brought you into His family and made you His child. That means you are a child of the King!

So what does that mean? It means you love God with all your heart. And you can trust Him completely. You don't have to be worried or afraid, because you know He will always take care of you. He even fills your heart with joy!

It also means you love Him so much that you want to obey Him. In the Bible, God tells His children things not to do, like lie, cheat and steal. But He tells us to do good things too—pray, share, love, be humble and kind.

When you remember you are God's child, you will want to live in a way that makes God—and others—happy.

You are a child of the King. That makes you a prince or a princess! So walk tall, smile big, and live like a child of God—because that's what you really are!

See what amazing love the Father has given us! Because of it, we are called children of God. And that's what we really are! (1 John 3:1 NIrV)

You Are God's Messenger

Have you ever received some really good news and you just couldn't wait to tell everyone about it? What's some good news you've shared? Maybe your team won a game, a fun party was coming up, a new baby joined your family or it was free ice cream cone day at your favorite shop!

We love sharing good things that are happening in our lives. And it's even better when it's something good for others too!

It's the same way when we know Jesus. He forgives our sins, gives us a wonderful, blessed life and promises us heaven one day. If we know Jesus, He's the *best news* of all! And that's Good News worth sharing! That's why Jesus tells us to go into the *whole world* and share the message of His Good News—because He wants others to come to Him too!

Ask God to show you different ways that you can spread the word about His Son, Jesus. Everyone deserves to hear about Him! Jesus gave each one of us this mission: to go into all the world and tell everyone His message of love. You're never too young or too old. God wants to use *you* to share this Good News with everyone. Remember—you are God's messenger!

And then he told them, "Go into all the world and preach the Good News to everyone." (Mark 16:15 NLT)

You Are Never Alone

Do you ever have to do something really hard and wonder how you're going to do it? We all face difficult things at one time or another. Maybe it's an assignment or a test at school. Maybe you're dealing with a bully. Or maybe there are some really big problems happening at home. You might wonder how you'll ever get through it.

Thankfully, whatever difficulties we face, we don't have to face them alone. God is always with us. He promises that when we go through deep waters, He will be with us. When we go through rivers of difficulty, we will not drown. And when we walk through a fiery trial, we will not be burned.

Whatever you are going through, God promises He will be with you. He will help you. He will protect you. You will make it through this—with Him.

The next time you face a difficult situation—or maybe you are right now—remember to call out to Jesus in prayer. Never forget that He is right there beside you—every step of the way. You are not alone. God is going to bring you through this!

When you go through deep waters, I will be with you. When you go through rivers of difficulty, you will not drown. When you walk through the fire of oppression, you will not be burned up; the flames will not consume you. (Isaiah 43:2 NLT)

You Are Protected

Do you ever feel a little afraid when the lights go out at night? Lots of kids do. Maybe you hear a creak in the house or see a shadow on the wall. Sometimes it makes your heart beat fast.

But you don't have to be afraid—because Jesus is with you, even in the dark. He is stronger than anything scary, and His love surrounds you like a warm, cozy blanket. When you whisper His name, you can know that He is right there, keeping you safe.

Nighttime is also not the time to worry. Worrying doesn't fix things—it just makes it harder to rest. Instead, you can give all your worries to Jesus.

Before you close your eyes, tell Him what's on your mind—every little fear, every problem, every person you care about. Then put it all in His hands. While you are sleeping, God is still working. He is strong, and He can take care of everything much better than you or I can! When you do this, your heart will feel peaceful, and your sleep will be sweet.

You are safe. You are protected. This is God's promise to you:

When you lie down, you will not be afraid; when you lie down, your sleep will be sweet. (Proverbs 3:24 NIV)

You Are Strong

Have you ever wished you had superpowers? We know superheroes aren't real, but it's fun to imagine them. Did you know God's power is greater than any superhero? There's no limit to His power. There's *nothing* He can't do!

God is all-powerful—no one is stronger than Him, not even the devil! He knows everything—nothing is hidden from Him. He can be everywhere at the same time—in a flash, He can come to your rescue! He has power over nature—Jesus calmed storms. He even has power over sickness and death—Jesus healed many people, and greatest of all, God raised Jesus from the dead!

The amazing part is that God wants to share His power with you. He wants to make you strong! I don't mean the kind of strength that lifts 1,000 pounds. God's strength is the kind that helps you keep going when life feels too hard. When others stumble and fall, His power will help you walk, run, and even soar high like an eagle.

If you put all your hope and trust in God, He will crown you with His strength and give you new power to live for Him. With God, you are strong!

But those who trust in the LORD will find new strength. They will soar high on wings like eagles. They will run and not grow weary. They will walk and not faint. (Isaiah 40:31 NLT)

You Are Considerate

Have you ever needed help with something? How did it feel when someone came to help you? Were you thankful?

Everybody likes people who are kind and considerate. Do you know what considerate means? It means thinking about what others need and helping make things easier for them. That's exactly what God wants us to do for one another—help each other carry our heavy loads.

What are some ways you can do that? Maybe you could help a friend with homework. Maybe you could share some money with someone who doesn't have enough. Maybe you could help an older neighbor with their yard work. Or maybe you could pray with someone who's going through a hard time, to help them feel better. There are so many ways to help others who are in need!

Ask God to show you how you can be helpful to people around you. Pray that He helps you be a cheerful giver—whether it's your time, your money or your talents. When you show kindness to others, you are doing what God wants you to do. And who knows? Maybe you'll help carry someone's load today, and another day, they'll help you carry yours!

Carry one another's heavy loads. If you do, you will fulfill the law of Christ. (Galatians 6:2 NIrV)

You Are Pushing Forward

Are you pressing toward your goal? If you belong to Jesus, a wonderful prize is waiting for you in heaven. You will live with Him forever! And if you do good things for God, you will also receive a crown—because you are a child of the King!

Life on earth isn't always easy. Following Jesus is like climbing a hill, you have to press on—keep pushing forward. If you stop, you might slip backward. That's why it's important to keep your eyes on Jesus and never give up!

There will be things that try to stop you. Temptations to do wrong. Hard times, like being sick or when others laugh at you for loving Jesus. Some people might try to make you believe things that don't match God's Word.

But God wants you to hold on to Him every day. If you mess up, you can ask Him to forgive you—and He will! God is on your side, cheering you on as you push forward to meet Him one day.

No matter what happens in your life, don't quit! Keep pressing on! Never let go of Jesus! Remember, there is a great prize waiting for you in heaven!

I press on toward the goal to win the prize for which God has called me heavenward in Christ Jesus. (Philippians 3:14 NIV)

You Are Growing Good Fruit

Have you ever tasted rotten fruit? It's slimy, it stinks, and it tastes awful. No one wants to eat rotten fruit—it might even make you sick!

Did you know that your life also produces fruit? What kind of fruit are you growing? Is it fresh and good? I sure hope it's not rotten and stinky!

If you love Jesus, the Holy Spirit grows good fruit in your life. But sometimes we forget to let Him do His work in us, and then our fruit can start to spoil.

Jesus said we are known by our fruit (Matthew 7:16). If our lives are full of lying, disobeying, or being unkind, that fruit tells others we aren't really following Jesus. But when we let the Holy Spirit lead us, our lives will grow beautiful fruit. When others see it, they will know that we love Jesus.

Ask God to show you what kind of fruit is coming from your life. If your fruit is starting to get rotten, ask the Holy Spirit to help you grow good fruit again. When people see your beautiful fruit, they'll want to be near you—and know more about Jesus! What kind of fruit are you growing today?

But the Holy Spirit produces this kind of fruit in our lives: love, joy, peace, patience, kindness, goodness, faithfulness, gentleness, and self-control. (Galatians 5:22–23 NLT)

You Are Mature

Have you ever been on a raft or a boat, riding the waves? It's so much fun to let the waves push you back and forth. But when it comes to our faith, God doesn't want us to be like a boat tossed around by the waves. He doesn't want us to stay spiritual babies. He wants us to grow up, learn His Word, and stand strong in our faith all of our lives.

That means if someone tells you something that isn't true about God, you won't just drift away and believe it. If someone wants you to do something you know is wrong, you won't let your "boat" be blown away from God.

Instead, you will be strong and immovable in God's truth. When someone tries to get you to believe—or do—something that goes against the Bible, you can stand firm and say, "No." That's called being spiritually mature. That's how you become more like Jesus.

Ask God to help you grow mature in your faith. Instead of being tossed back and forth by wrong ideas, put your anchor in Jesus. He will keep you from drifting away when people try to turn you from God's truth.

...become mature...Then we will no longer be infants, tossed back and forth by the waves, and blown here and there by every wind of teaching and by the cunning and craftiness of people in their deceitful scheming. (Ephesians 4:13-14 NIV)

You Are Chosen

Do you know that you were hand-picked by God to be His own special treasure? You are more valuable to God than diamonds, silver or gold. He says you are like a royal crown in His hand! (Isaiah 62:3)

Some days you may not feel very special. Maybe you were the last one picked on the team. Maybe kids even fought because they didn't want *you* on their team! Don't worry, God always wants you on His team. He will choose you every. single. time.

God holds you close to His heart—because you are His treasure! He protects you. He doesn't want anyone to steal you away from Him.

He polishes you, too—helping your heart stay shiny and clean. We're like silver that sometimes has imperfections. When that happens, God gently rubs those flaws away until He can see the reflection of His face in us again.

As God's treasure, you don't have to worry about what anyone else in this world says about you. All that matters is what God says: You are valuable to Him. You are special. You are His treasure. God has chosen *you*!

The LORD your God has chosen you to be his own special treasure. (Deuteronomy 7:6 NLT)

You Are Blessed

Do you want the Lord's face to shine on you? Do you want Him to bless your life in wonderful ways? If you do, the first step is to seek Him.

There are lots of things people try to find in this world. Some look for fame. Others want money, fun, or excitement. But none of those things truly make us happy, because what we really need most is to look for God—and His Son, Jesus.

Sadly, some people turn away from God, instead of looking for Him. When they do, it's like they're pushing Him away—His love, His protection, His goodness, and His blessings. Why would anyone ever want to do that?

I pray that you will always follow God—with all your heart. When you do, He will bless you and keep you safe. He will smile on you and take special care of you as you go through life. With His hand on you, you don't need to be afraid. He will fill your heart with peace.

This is the blessing I pray for you...today and every day of your life:

The Lord bless you and keep you; the Lord make his face shine on you and be gracious to you; the Lord turn his face toward you and give you peace. (Numbers 6:24-26 NIV)

You Are Extra-Ordinary

Do you believe God can do *anything*? Do you believe God can do anything through *you*? You are no ordinary child. You are *extra-ordinary*! God has called you to be a world-changer!

You might be thinking, "But I'm nothing special. I'm just an ordinary kid." Well, remember the boy in the Bible who gave Jesus his tiny meal of a few fish and loaves of bread? When he gave them to Jesus, a miracle happened—Jesus used that little bit of food to feed over 5,000 hungry people!

Your life is like that boy's tiny meal. On your own, you might feel ordinary, but this is what happens when you put your life in Jesus' hands: YOU + JESUS = **EXTRA**-ORDINARY!

Give your whole life to Jesus. Ask Him to use you to do great things for Him. Believe Him for the impossible. If God says something in His Word, trust Him—He will do it! Jesus says that if you believe, *all things* are possible!

Who knows what God is going to do through your life? With Jesus, you are never just ordinary—you are ***extra*-*ordinary***!

Jesus said to him, "If you can believe, all things are possible to him who believes." (Mark 9:23 NKJV)

Look for these future books by Angela Forker:

You Are Not Alone: Declaring God's Reassuring Word Over Your Children

You Are a Masterpiece: Declaring God's Flourishing Word Over Your Unborn Child

You Are Courageous: Declaring God's Victorious Word Over Your Children

You Are Valuable: Declaring God's Affirming Word Over Your Child with Special Needs

I'd love to hear from you!

Contact me at: angelaforker@outlook.com

You may also be interested in this book for adults:

Walking with the Shepherd: Inspirational Stories from the Pasture

Check out Angela's photography at:

www.preciousbabyphotography.com